Water from Wellspring

From the Congregation of Wellspring United Methodist Church

Williamsburg, VA

 Blue Dragon Publishing

Water from Wellspring
From the Congregation of Wellspring United Methodist
Church
Williamsburg, VA

All rights reserved.
Published by Blue Dragon Publishing, LLC
www.blue-dragon-publishing.com
Copyright 2018 Wellspring United Methodist Church

Cover by Resa Reid
Editor: Paige Brotherton

ISBN 978-1-939696-40-3 (paperback)
ISBN 978-1-939696-41-0 (eBook)
Library of Congress Control Number: 2018946734

The Scripture quotations contained herein are from the
New Revised Standard Version Bible, copyright © 1989,
by the Division of Christian Education of the National
Council of the Churches of Christ in the U.S.A. Used by
permission. All rights reserved.

Printed in the U.S.A.

Table of Contents

Introduction	5
All Things Work Together for Good	7
Let HIStory be Our Story	11
God has a Plan	20
Blessed by God	35
This Little Light of Mine	39
Communion: Intimate Communication	46
Finding God in the Unexpected	58
The Road to Methodism	65
One Thing Leads to Another	72
Saved by Angels	76
What Does Jesus Look Like?	86
God's Will	97
When the Moon Blocked out the Son	101
No Ah-ha Moment	105
Share Your Story	112

Introduction

Wellspring United Methodist Church is a medium-size church tucked into the trees off of Longhill Road in Williamsburg, Virginia. The parking lot is only partially paved, there are no bells, and the steeple doesn't rise above the treetops.

But it's what's on the inside that counts.

This loving and welcoming church has opened its doors to visitors, members, and people who have attended regularly for almost 40 years. Their outreach has included food pantries, habitat houses, youth fellowship, mission trips, Stephen Ministry, and the Sewing Sisters.

Like most churches, attendance is greatest around Easter and Christmas, but the faithful church-goers come back Sunday after Sunday to ensure the doors remain open for those that come by when they need to.

Recently, the pastor at Wellspring focused his sermons around telling HIStory—Jesus' story. Now the congregation would like to share their stories of Christian love through the pages of this book. By sharing their stories of how Christ has moved in their lives, the communicants hope to stir memories and reminders of how Christ has moved—and continues to move—in the lives of the readers.

Remember to share your story of Jesus's love with the world.

All Things Work Together for Good

by Joyce Huffman

Beginning with the moment of your birth, each of us has a story to tell. Your story is unique because there is only one you. But upon reflection, one might consider a series of events not as coincidences, but rather, God surrounding you with people who may interact to allow a Spiritual Gift to grow to His purpose.

In my case, it was the congregation of California United Methodist Church in California, Pennsylvania in the 1960s.

To this day, I'm amazed that a woman who neither sang nor played the piano gave me a gift of sheet music; that the previous church choir director was in attendance that Sunday morning and generously responded to my distress; and that a simple knock on the door was an act of compassion and mission.

Your Spiritual Gifts are not given for your own benefit, but for the benefit of others. Every ministry matters because we all depend on others to function and to share.

All things work together for good for those who love the Lord.

"What if I fall? Oh, but my darling, what if you fly?"

I FALL

As a new member of the congregation and the choir, I had agreed to sing a duet with our tenor choir director. It was a rather easy selection but with a repetitive half note that challenged my range four times. Was it a G? Memory fails me. I do know I missed it the first time, confirming my fear that I was going to miss it three more times. The trouble with duets or solos is that you must sing on until the music ends and you can sit down.

My distress must have been so obvious, because following the service, I was showered with encouragement and compliments. I asked my husband to please take me home, for if one more person was nice to me, I was going to cry.

We were home only a short time when a neighbor knocked on the screen door. Mr. Halstead, head of the music department at the local college, wanted to help me. He would give me free voice lessons, and we would work together preparing something special for a return engagement at California United Methodist Church.

I FLY

For the next three months I knocked on Mr. Halstead's door once a week. What a sight greeted him. I had my three little ones, a few toys, and a piece of sheet music, *Consider the Lilies*, which I had received as a gift. "Will this do?"

"Yes," he answered simply.

I promised to practice at home every day by repeating that week's lesson on my own. I neither played nor had a piano. The neighbors would just have to put up with me.

After months of practice, Mr. Halstead determined it was time. "Joyce, you're ready. After you sing, the congregation can rise and go home. The sermon will have been delivered," he told me.

Knowing I was nervous and under self-imposed pressure, Mr. Halstead comforted me by saying he would stand at the rear of the sanctuary under the beautiful stained-glass window. I could project to him but sing to the congregation.

It's now 50 years later, and I can still sing that solo in my mind—every breath, every inflection, every rest, every nuance, every note. There was even a G.

I FLEW

Let HIStory be Our Story

By Edward Hopkins

My parents insisted that I be in Sunday school and church every Sunday until I graduated from high school. We lived in Roanoke, Virginia. In 1974, I moved to Williamsburg to begin studies at William and Mary, and, beginning my junior year, I took a room at the Wesley Foundation on Jamestown Road, next-door to the big Methodist Church.

That year I took an Old Testament survey class taught by Dr. Hans Tiefel. The class proved to be one of the most intriguing classes I had while I was a student. I discovered in that class that, despite growing up in Sunday school and church, I really had not learned anything about the incredible stories in the Bible. I mean, I had listened to them read and preached, but I had never *heard* them.

Hear, O Israel: The Lord is our God, the Lord alone. You shall love the Lord your God with all your heart, and with all your soul, and with all your might. Keep these words that I am commanding you today in your heart. Recite them to your children and talk about them when you are at home and when you are away, when you lie down and when you rise. Bind them as a sign on your hand, fix them as an emblem on your forehead, and write them on the doorposts of your house and on your gates (Deuteronomy 6:4-9).

The Torah insists that the story of God's redeeming love be told to the children over and over and over—that they listen to the story over and over and over—until they hear it. Then, because of the parents' persistence, the children are given the opportunity to fall in love with the God of Abraham, Isaac, and Jacob.

I remember leaving Dr. Tiefel's class one afternoon, coming back to my room at the Wesley Foundation, and, gathered with several

Wesley students, sharing my excitement about what I had just learned. I sat on my bed and told everyone how Abraham, who was as old as dust, heard from some strangers one day who had come by his tent that his wife, Sarah, who was almost as old as dust, would give birth to a child in a year. The suggestion was so ridiculous that Sarah, who overheard the comment, could not restrain a scornful laugh. She must have thought, "What? I have been barren for ninety years—not able to do the *one thing* a woman is supposed to do to be useful—and now I am going to have a baby? Really? You make me laugh." All the servants laughed at the thought. Abraham even laughed.

The next year, Sarah had a baby! She laughed for joy so hard she almost cried! The Lord had opened her womb and Abraham and Sarah named the child Isaac, a Hebrew word which means "laughing."

I told everyone in the room that day, that if I ever had a son, I was going to name him Isaac! A young woman named Janet (for whom I was developing a serious crush) was in the room.

Everything came crashing to a halt for me when, in December 1977, I suffered the last migraine headache I would ever have and fell unconscious on the floor of my room at the Wesley House. My roommate called the ambulance and I was rushed to the hospital. I was diagnosed with adult on-set hydrocephalus. Over the next eight months I had four brain operations to install shunts—small plastic valves that allowed fluid to exit my head and be deposited elsewhere in my body.

I spent three months in the hospital fighting for my life and a month in a medically induced coma. I had speech, occupational, and physical therapy for four months, and then was blessed to return to William and Mary in February 1979.

I graduated in May, and Janet and I were married a year later. However, believing my hydrocephalus to be a congenital problem, Janet and I decided that we would not have children; would not risk passing a disease to our offspring. For eight years we were married, happy, and childless.

In 1988, as I sat beside our newborn son in the hospital nursery, I looked at his perfect little fingers and toes and at his perfectly hydrocephalus-free head, and I started to laugh.

Janet and I named him Isaac, a Hebrew word which means "laughing."

Janet spent hours and hours holding, cuddling, and rocking Isaac. She talked to him constantly and read to him without end. I enjoyed my opportunities to hold Isaac also, rocking him and reading to him from a little Bible picture book that was one of his favorites. I read to him, over and over, the story of Abraham, Sarah, and their little son named Isaac. The book had a large, colorful picture of the happy family.

When Isaac was about ten months old, I had prayers with him one night, put him in his crib, placed his Bible picture book in the crib with him (because he wouldn't go to sleep without it), turned off his light, and pulled his bedroom door almost closed. I went to bed.

Janet and I woke up in the middle of the night for some reason, and we noticed a light on in Isaac's room. We got up, crept down the hallway and looked through the crack in Isaac's doorway. Isaac had evidently pulled himself up in the crib, reached the switch, and turned on the lights. We watched as Isaac sat studying carefully the picture of Abraham, Sarah, and

Isaac in his Bible book. With his little finger he traced the faces depicted on the page and spoke quietly to himself. His words were just unintelligible sounds, of course, but I have no doubt that he was telling himself the story of Abraham and Sarah and their little boy whom they named Isaac, a Hebrew word which means "laughing!"

I was held and rocked as a child, and my parents told me the story of who I was. My parents were both rocked and told the story, as were their parents and their grandparents and on and on. Suzanna Wesley rocked her children and told them the story of God's redemptive plan for humanity.

> Jesus was rocked by Mary,
> Moses was rocked by Jochebed,
> Joseph was rocked by Rachel...

There is something immensely comforting about being held in loving arms and rocked gently. Maybe it reminds us of the security we had as we were ensconced in the womb's cocoon:

the rhythmic heart beats,
the whoosh of the blood,
the swaying back and forth
as our mother moved about.
Everything is going to be alright.

There is something immensely comforting about being rocked and told the story of who we are and whose we are. Our story is of a God whose thundering voice calls into being a rhythm and an order that overcame, overcomes, and will always overcome the forces of chaos, disorder, darkness, and death in the world. God's narrative begins with an enduring refrain in Genesis 1:

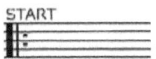

God said...
let there be...
and there was...
and God said, "It is good!"
and there was evening and morning...
and everything is going to be alright...
and when everything is not alright
and when life goes out of rhythm,

God made a seventh day HOLY
God said, "CLEAR!"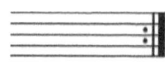
Repeat the refrain…

That is why we have decided to tell the story of our faith with great care in 2017 and beyond. The Wellspring United Methodist congregation is scattered all over everywhere all week long. Our lives are always shifting; every day we face new struggles, new setbacks, new problems, and new difficulties. Chaos always seems perched, ready to make life meaningless. In a moment, our lives can explode into disparate pieces by a late-night visit from the state police, or a doctor's diagnosis, or an angry conversation with a spouse that ends in a walk out, or a "Dear John" letter, or the reception of an unsuspected pink slip…

But on the seventh day, like clockwork, God's people enter the worship space, and I slip into the rocking chair. We listen for God's story—the predictable, familiar, comfortable rhythm that makes life coherent. The Story of God is the way that we humans can begin to make sense of our chaos, to recollect our identities, and put our lives back together again. Then, we can go back into the world living out God's Story and serving God's purposes.

God has a Plan

By Stan Yackel

When Pastor Edward requested our Congregation help him with the theme "Everyone Has a Story," it seemed to be a simple task to put our life story into words. Now that it's time to put words on paper, accomplishing that task isn't anywhere as easy as I thought, and I now realize how making My Story interesting is a real challenge. So I need to manage your expectations and caution you to not expect anything significant. Please don't measure this "message" against the others that have presented a much more interesting story. Deal? Okay, let's get started.

WHY TELL THIS STORY? I am not going to try and convert you to anything or persuade you to change your attitude about how you feel God plans our future or knows what we'll be doing before we do. But, I am hopeful you will understand how my life experiences have brought me to believe that God *does* influence our decisions and that He *has* a plan for us. Each of you has your own story about the many decisions and circumstances that have brought us to this place together today...my hope is you, too, will reflect sometime on your major life decisions and events and see how God wants to help you succeed along your path.

Of course, as the old adage says, "hindsight is always 20-20," and that's a good thing when evaluating where God has been actively guiding me on this journey.

IN THE BEGINNING: (At least beginning when God started bringing people and events into my life that set the course for later on) Unequivocally, the best thing that ever happened to me has been my childhood sweetheart and wife of 50 years, Mary. For those of you that know her, you understand exactly what I mean. She is clearly the *better* half. You will understand more when you read her story.

Our story began when she was five and I was eight...hmmm, that's almost 70 years ago. We were introduced in her uncle's backyard at a gathering for the new minister, my dad, to their church in Lodi, California. We kids were playing as kids do, making up games. The next thing we knew, someone ran to the adults and exclaimed, "Reverend Yackel, come quick. You need to marry Mary and Stanley. They love each other."

A pretend game of course, but what a first impression on his new congregation. They thought it was pretty funny, but poor Mary took the brunt of that pretend game when her parents got her home.

Little did we know then that God was already guiding our paths, because we would end up in a marriage that has lasted over 50 years, so far, and is clearly a work in progress. So parents, watch for those early friendships, because you never know what they will lead to. More importantly, pick the friends you want your kids to be around, even at an early age.

Out of this early beginning, came the best gift God could have ever given us, our daughter Michelle.

OUR FIRST CHALLENGE: Since our marriage came in the middle of my college career, and Michelle came along during that time, our first life-changing decision was to see if I could finish college. God blessed us with many miracles in those early years including well-paying part-time jobs that kept us on track for me to finish with a degree in Aero Engineering. Recounting the times when it looked like dropping out would be far easier and the prudent thing to do, there was, somehow, a path laid forward for us to follow that got us through. We have never stopped thanking our gracious God for the support He provided during those times. We certainly weren't clever enough on our own to meet that challenge.

But challenges in life continue throughout. During the late 1960s, this country was in a period of calling our young people into the military service and sending them to Vietnam. Well, after two years of an initial career designing aircraft with McDonnell Douglas in Long Beach, California, I had more surprises in store for Mary. Working around former military pilots that were testing our aircraft and having several good friends that went off to fly in the military following college, my patriotic duty seemed to get the best of me. That was the first time in my life when I experienced the dilemma as to whether these were my own selfish decisions, or if I was following the will of God in what to do next.

OUR BIG CHALLENGE: We had recently purchased our first house. One day, I came home to explain to my happy wife and sweet, little four-year-old, that I had talked to an Air Force recruiter, and he was offering me a chance to fly jets. You can probably imagine her disbelief that I would even consider this. That's a kind way to say she thought I was nuts. Especially since we loved our church and new friends in Huntington Beach, California. As illogical as it seemed, we did pray about this decision and talked to my uncle (an Army colonel) and our folks. But now comes the first of many instances where there was no burning bush or voice calling out to me in the night or any other crystal-clear message from God that says, "Go follow your dream!"

So how do we determine the right course of action for decisions that have life altering outcomes? How do we know if that action is consistent with what God wants for us?

Well, for me, I struggled. I would wake up in the night with sweaty palms, looking for signs, trying to discuss with Mary objectively (which seemed to continue endlessly) and sometimes in not very friendly terms.

But ultimately, I had to decide, and then we faced the next chapter in our lives—still uncertain if it was one I selfishly followed or if it was the will of God. Would He continue to bless me if I didn't follow His will? Would He take away His blessing if I was wrong?

FAST FORWARD TWO YEARS: My dream came true. I was a fighter pilot, having graduated high enough in my class to get my first choice of aircraft—the F-4 Phantom, the premier fighter back in the day. However, the fulfillment of my dream wasn't so exciting for my supportive wife when she found out that choice meant a 10-month course learning how to fly combat, followed by a pipeline to Vietnam.

You might wonder how she handled the fear she had about the separation and dangers associated with flying combat when we were beginning to lose aircraft and pilots over North Vietnam at an alarming rate. Well, she relied on the strength of our Christian upbringing and privately started her prayer vigil for God to intervene and find another way for us to continue our military service doing the thing I loved.

Imagine my surprise when our class was the first one that wouldn't let new lieutenants go directly to Vietnam without an operational assignment first to gain more experience. And, of course, she let me know that this clearly was an answer to her prayers of the last 10 months.

So, off to Spain we went for four years and many wonderful experiences, and we were together. This was Mary's reassurance that God does listen to our prayers, and it helped her become a faithful follower of that belief throughout these many years. It became totally apparent to us that God has a plan—even when it appears we are making selfish choices.

This real-life, answer-to-prayer experience became the standard for our 20-year career in the Air Force and the many choices that came our way as we faced where our life would lead us. When faced with difficult decisions, we trusted God to help show us the way.

ANOTHER OBVIOUS EXAMPLE: While stationed at Langley Air Force Base and living in Poquoson, Virginia, we committed to leading the youth group at Tabernacle United

Methodist Church. This was out of desperation to keep Michelle, our eighth grader, involved. She said she hated going to church as the new kid and had no friends there. We wanted her to get to know others her age. We decide to make it fun for the kids in the Methodist Youth Fellowship Group while giving them a little spiritual guidance mixed in—it worked! Not only did it work for her, but we met a great teenage boy that loved sports and outdoor stuff like I did. We quickly decided he was the cream of the crop and redouble our efforts to keep the youth group together.

This became the answer to our prayer that she would love going to church activities and would find her strength through a relationship with Jesus Christ. We believed Jesus would eventually lead her to the man of her dreams. Kenny Forrest answered that call, and he ultimately became our son-in-law. He is the kind of guy I would have picked to be my very own son, if I had the choice.

I asked myself the question, was God guiding us or were we just lucky? Now we look back and know, beyond a shadow of doubt, that God has a plan, as long as we listen and keep

Him as the center of our life. The scripture that has come to mean so much to me through the years comes from Joshua speaking to the Israelites in Joshua 24:15, "As for me and my house, we will serve the Lord."

HOW DO WE WEATHER THE STORMS? Every marriage and family goes through struggles. Obviously, life in the military has its built-in challenges. One is many days, months, and years of separation from our families. Ours was no exception. The many months of deployments while in Europe were not easy, but Mary developed an independence of operation that got us through, somehow. The military has certain places where families can't travel with the member; these are considered remote assignments. My remote assignment was to Iceland, chasing Russian aircraft that came through NATO airspace. They liked to pretend they were attacking Iceland with their bombers or chasing our submarines in the North Atlantic Ocean, and we would scramble to intercept them, regardless of the weather conditions. This was to let them know that we were ready if they ever decided it wasn't just a game.

Following that year apart came one of our hardest decisions that we made as a family. Michelle was a junior in high school and doing well. The Air Force decided to send me to Command and Staff College following my year in Iceland. Being selected was a good deal for my career, but unfortunately it was in Alabama. Many prayers later, we decided to suck it up for another 10 months and leave Mary and Michelle in Poquoson for Michelle to finish her senior year. A tough decision, but one we will never regret. Out of that sacrifice, Michelle continued to thrive, go to college, and finally seal the deal with her Kenny Forrest after seven patient years of dating and waiting for that special time to be together as husband and wife. Was that just a lucky decision for our family? I think not, and I will always believe that out of our humanness, He will guide our paths to a wonderful outcome. Yes, God has a plan, if we will only dial him into our decisions, no matter how small or insignificant they seem.

FOLLOWING THOSE GLORIOUS AIR FORCE YEARS: After retirement from the Air Force, we were faced with a decision about what to do next. More prayers, more choices, more projecting what we thought was the right thing to do. The answer: We headed to Georgia and a great job with Lockheed Martin helping with the development of new airplanes, including the F-22 Raptor, and other projects for the military. This second career was a time for making great friends and worshiping in the Acworth United Methodist Church. We continued to build on our Christian foundations and learned more about how our merciful God works in such mysterious ways.

The highlight of this time happened early on, with the birth of our first grandchild. Our dear little Megan is now a Lieutenant Junior Grade Officer in the Navy. We took many trips to North Carolina to watch her grow, and then a couple of years later, more blessings came with the arrival of her brother, Tyler—now a 6' 5" child of God who has graduated from Old Dominion University. The time we spent with them is cherished memories now, as many with grandkids can understand. Both grandkids are now married to wonderful spouses whom we adore and who are making Godly decisions in the paths they choose in their young lives.

This chapter of our lives in Georgia was a refreshing change for us by getting to stay in one house and one location, for the longest time we had experienced in our married life...over 14 years. For those of you that have had more stability in your life, it's probably hard to imagine moving as often as we did, but it did give us a spirit of adventure in knowing that relocating and finding new friends can be a very rewarding experience.

So when an opportunity came to think about an early retirement from Lockheed, we were thinking how wonderful it would be to be close enough to our daughter's family to enjoy the grandkids as they went through their school years at home. More prayer, more sleepless nights, more wondering if this was our human selfishness in wanting to do something we wanted or was this part of God helping us decide. It was during this period that I discovered one of my all-time favorite verses in the Bible. I'm sure some of you know it by heart; it comes from the Old Testament from the book of Jeremiah 29:11. "'For I know the plans I have for you,' declares the Lord, 'plans to prosper you and not to harm you, plans to give you hope and a future.'" Now many years later, there is no doubt in my mind that, as we look back at where we have been, **GOD HAD A PLAN and it was up to us to continue living in His will.**

SO HERE WE ARE: After 12 years at Lake Anna watching our grandkids grow up and enjoying the wonderful people in the Mineral/Mt. Pleasant United Methodist Church, we were looking for the next chapter in our lives and wondering if God was calling us to another wonderful congregation. Now we find ourselves enjoying this next season in our lives by getting to know and appreciate the Christian brothers and sisters at Wellspring United Methodist Church in beautiful Williamsburg, VA.

It's incredible to reflect on these last 70 years and see how God's hand has been instrumental in helping to create so many treasured memories--traveling with friends, experiencing the graduations of our grandkids, and being close enough to watch the influence God has had guiding Kenny and Michelle through the challenges of parenthood. The joy continues as we watch their family grow through the addition of another Navy Lieutenant Junior

Grade Charlie Graham, taking over the responsibility of our own Lieutenant Junior Grade Megan through a marriage that we all know God ordained. And our grandson, Tyler, marrying his longtime high school sweetheart, Kerrie Chisholm. Did the prayers we offered throughout their lives have an effect on their choices of a life partner? I believe prayer is one of those wonderful gifts you can give your children and grandchildren, for those of you that have been blessed with these gifts.

IN CONCLUSION: As we enter this next season of our lives, we pray God will continue guiding us though the valleys and mountain top experiences that we all experience in our lives. We have been blessed way beyond what we deserve, and we thank God for all He has provided. I am delighted that our path is now intersecting with yours and realize that our prayers continue to be answered as we serve Him in whatever ways we are being led. We know that life is filled with surprises and uncertainty, but we remain confident in the promises that God has given us through the Bible and the gift of His Son Jesus Christ. One day I look forward to a complete understanding of my claim that **GOD HAS A PLAN!**

Blessed by God

by Mary Yackel

My faith journey began even before I knew what faith was. I didn't know a lot about Jesus (except lessons from Sunday school) because I was only five years old.

I loved my parents and big sister, but there was always so much stress at home. My dad owned his own business and worked very hard—too hard—to show others how successful he was with only a sixth-grade education. He had always wanted sons to help in the business, but he got two girls, seven and a half years apart.

A new minister and his family moved to our church in August of 1952. They had an 11-year-old daughter, 8-year-old son, and a baby girl. I saw such happiness and joy in this family, then went home to my *hidden* life—perfect on the outside but something different when we were alone. I felt so insecure and afraid all the time. Divorce was a constant threat with yelling and horrible scenes.

I looked forward to Sundays because I loved the feeling at church. We would eat out often with church friends and the minister's family. I got to spend time with Stanley, the minister's son, who I had a huge crush on even at the age of five and six; he was three years older. These were some of my happiest memories as a kid. At that time, my parents seemed so happy. My dad was always funny and generous, and he loved being the center of attention.

Then we went home to our *hidden* life of threats and fear of the unknown. This went on for many years. When I was ten years old, my sister got married in a huge, lavish wedding. She was back home in four months. Then a lot more stress came into our lives. Still, from the outside we looked like the perfect middle-class, Christian family. It got harder and harder for me to understand why other families seemed so different. I especially was drawn to our minister's family.

I accepted Jesus into my life at 13 at church camp in Mission Springs, California. Church camp was always the best week of summer. I could begin to feel like the other kids, and Stan was at camp, too. Then I went home...

I prayed a lot for things to change. It never seemed to go in a positive direction. As I got older and began driving, I spent as much time away from home as I could. My best friend, Candy, had a loving, happy family even when times were tough for them. I spent many weekends with them. I wanted desperately to tell them about my life at home, but I was too afraid. I still felt my love growing for Stan, even when he was away for two years at college.

I was 17 and Stan was 20 when we got married by his father in their living room with my parents and a few guests from Iowa.

Life was still not easy with Stan in college for two more years and working part time, but there was the unconditional love I had never experienced. God gave us our beautiful, perfect daughter, and we had more love than we knew was possible. God helped raise that infant through some scary times; He was always with us. Stan's father baptized her at three months, and she has always been God's child. She has brought more love and joy to us these 50 plus years through her husband and their two amazing children. Now those grandchildren, along with their wonderful spouses, bring even more love into our lives through their extended families. We cherish and feel blessed with each of these relationships!

I know now God was with me growing up, but I didn't have a close relationship with Him. It took time, maturity, and life experiences to truly trust Him. I have felt his real presence several times in my life and those times will never leave me; they have been reinforced by trust.

Stan's sisters are two of my very best friends in life. They are two of the most faithful, strong Christians I've ever known. I didn't just marry the love of my life, I married into the family that has always shown me unconditional love in the purest way.

God has truly loved me, guided me along the way, and BLESSED me!

This Little Light of Mine

By Paige Brotherton

Last June, at age 15, I was confirmed as a child of God and a member of Wellspring United Methodist Church. It was a big decision and a beautiful ceremony, but the two did not happen in the same place. The ceremony, of course, took place in the chapel; but my decision to become a Christian took place in an IHOP parking lot.

    I have been a Christian for the majority of my childhood, mainly because my mom is a Christian who read the Bible to me and brought me to church every Sunday. Even when logic and that science-thing that schools teach tried to subtly hint to me that my current belief system had some holes, I stood my ground to the outside world of doubt. I was looking forward to the confirmation classes where I would get to really question my faith and make it stronger by having someone answer all my questions.

Confirmation is an amazing and wonderful and enlightening experience that I think everyone and anyone would love to do if they had a chance. Even if you can't get a class, find a mentor. Having someone to talk to, just someone to hear my beliefs and to learn from, was the most influential part of confirmation for me.

One thing confirmation doesn't do, however, is answer all your questions. Only God can do that. But my need for answers that no one could provide was weakening my faith.

I said in my creed when I joined the church that my wonderful mentor, Ms. BJ, saved a Christian. She sat through my thousands of questions and never made me feel like my doubting or curiosity was bad. In the end, the last week of confirmation, she was the first to guess that I was seriously debating, not only whether to join the church, but whether or not I wanted to continue my life as a Christian. I had actually been thinking about it for almost a year. Most people might not guess that about me. I never acted like someone who was considering leaving the church forever. But I was.

After all the retreats and official meetings, Ms. BJ and I had one last meeting before Confirmation Sunday.

We talked for a while, and Ms. BJ gave me one more day to make the decision. I promised to text her the next morning, and we walked out of the restaurant together. I said goodbye, realizing in that moment that my answer was no. After the classes, lessons, and church Sundays, I just felt like my faith was empty without the answers. I decided that the God I'd been singing about, learning about, and even talking to, was nothing more than something impossible that I'd grown up believing in. I decided, in that parking lot, not to be a Christian.

The ceremony of confirmation welcomes us into the church, but entering into God's kingdom can happen anywhere. All it takes is a sincere choice and an acceptance of God's love and reality. But leaving God's kingdom can happen anywhere, too. All it takes is a sincere choice and a refusal to accept God's love and reality. I made that choice last June.

I wouldn't say it was the worst choice I've ever made. Far from it, actually. Because I got to experience something I never had before: what it was like to not be a Christian.

I thought I'd been empty with my unanswered questions. I had no idea.

One of my childhood friends loved to sing a song that goes, "This little light of mine, I'm going to let it shine." I love that song and what it means; the grace of Jesus Christ, the love of God, and the fellowship of the Holy Spirit was shining out of every Christian onto every one of God's children, whether they knew where the light was coming from or not. Two seconds after I'd made the decision not be a Christian, it was like a little light in my heart clicked off. No rumble of thunder, no angry bellow from heaven, no world turned upside-down. Just a little click, and a part of my heart went dark.

Then I truly felt empty. I felt alone, too, in a way I never have before. God never left me, I've always known that. Just because I decided I didn't love Him anymore didn't mean He stopped loving me. He never has, and he never will.

In Isaiah 55, God is clear about His everlasting covenant and faithful love that will never end. There have been times in my life when I didn't pray enough. I didn't try my best when someone needed me. I didn't love others as much as I should have. I've been lost and distant from God and in serious need of a spiritual reset button, but God never left me feeling empty. He was willing to stay right by me through every moment up until I stood up and said I wanted out. Now I know what empty feels like.

I can no longer say I've been a Christian all my life. Because for ten seconds, in an IHOP parking lot, I was not a Christian. Ten seconds. That's how long it took me to realize how I wanted to live, and more importantly, how God wanted me to live.

I stopped walking towards my dad, who was waiting in the car, and I turned around and started back towards Ms. BJ.

"I want to be a Christian," I said loudly.

She smiled and said, "Yes? Are you sure?"

I nodded and said something like "Yep. Definitely."

It wasn't because all my questions had suddenly been answered. It wasn't because I didn't know what I would do on Sundays without church. It was because I couldn't stand to leave that place without God in my soul. I didn't want to have a dark place in my heart when it could be brighter than the Valley of Lights.

In Isaiah 55:11, God speaks of His plans and faith in us. "So shall my word be that goes out from my mouth; it shall not return to me empty but it shall accomplish that which I purpose, and succeed in the thing for which I sent it." God believes in us and has raised us to shine our lights in ways that promote the love of Jesus Christ.

I want to spend the rest of my life sharing my light with people who need it. I want to sing in ways that move to people. I want to help others in a way that makes people want to pass kindness forward. I even want to tell my story, tell God's story, and turn the *So What Corner* in a way that brightens people's faith.

I plan to keep shining God's light on the unsuspecting people of the world, and, with

Jesus's help, I will never let my light go out again.

Communion: Intimate Communication

By Connie Reitz

My prayer:
May my telling of this story—of Your story in my life—be heard with open hearts and minds. If it resonates with someone, may it stay with them. If not, may it gently roll away without affecting their faith. Amen

We've started on a new theme of study at Wellspring, making HIStory our story and sharing it with others. I like it. What is the story of Jesus, the story of Jesus in my life, the story I share with others? How did my story start, meander, change, evolve? How do I share this story with others—or do I?

This is my part of HIStory, and I tell it through communion.

One day I was thinking about communion—the rite, the ritual, the service, the table. Now this was long before Pastor Edward had approached me to share a message with the congregation. This was after listening to one of his sermons and trying to understand what HIStory is in my story.

I was thinking back to the church I was reared in, a small southern Baptist church. It was a beautiful place with exposed dark wooden beams which formed arches and triangles that held the roof off our heads. Heavy, opaque, milk-glass lights hung—or dangled depending on your state of youthful mind and boredom—from long metal chains. There were tall, glorious, stained-glass windows. It was good.

It was where I was baptized in a pool under the stained-glass picture of Jesus asking the children to come to him. I was nine years old. I participated in my first communion service sitting on the curved front pew with Emily, Janet, and Patricia—the three other girls my age who had been baptized the same day as me.

About three years later, a new sanctuary was built. The old sanctuary became the chapel. The stained-glass window of Jesus seeking the children was moved above the choir pews. The new sanctuary was a soaring modern place with seafoam green walls and white woodwork. The windows were clear glass. The pews had pads and were straight as an arrow. Communion was always on the first Sunday of the month.

Twelve men stood up from different areas of the church—wherever they happened to be seated with their families—and came forward. These were the deacons. They all wore white shirts, suits, ties, and dark shoes. It was an orchestrated ritual. They formed a semi-circle around the table, received a plate of bread, turned, and uniformly went to a specific pew to serve the bread. The plate was offered to the first person at the end of the pew. He or she took it and handed it to the person next to them, so that the first person could take a piece of bread. And so it continued down the line until all were served.

When the deacons returned the plates, the minister would serve these 12 men. The minister would announce to the congregation, "Take this bread and eat it." Everyone would place the small piece of bread in their mouth.

Then the same procedure was repeated with the cup—individual, tiny, glass cups in a heavy metal tray. This was the way it was done. I felt it took forever, until I became old enough to realize this time of waiting for all to be served was a time for me. I could close my eyes, I could pray, I could be thankful, and I could celebrate events past or things to come. It was good to be quiet with God.

My life progressed, I went to school, I lived in other states, and for a brief time, overseas. I met Jack, and we shared a growing, trusting relationship. We tried going to each other's church and found we both liked his—Hidenwood Presbyterian. We were married there, and our son Stephen was baptized there. I grew to love the people of that church, and my life was good. We went on trips with the youth, got to know church camps again, and were a part of the church.

Communion was served in much the same way I was used to, except now women were participating in the service; there was a female assistant minister. It was good. Except for that one time.

It was communion. Two rows did not get served the bread—I happened to be in one of those rows. The attention of one of the servers was caught, and he came back to serve those two rows, or so I thought. Only the row in front of me was served. I was devastated. Do I stand up and announce, "Not all have been served"? I didn't.

When the cup was served, everyone was included, but my heart had been broken. I left for home so sad. I have never been sad after receiving communion. How could this be? The tears came. I was angry at the deacons who forgot us, but also at myself for not speaking up. Well, it would never happen again. Monday morning meant a visit to the church with a detailed explanation of the events of the prior day's service. From then and until the last time I attended that church and communion was offered, the question was asked before anyone took the bread or cup, "Have all been served?" My heart was happy. Never again would someone seeking to share in communion with God be forgotten.

Then we moved to Williamsburg, Virginia and decided we'd go to the Presbyterian church in which Jack had been reared and his mother attended still. Whoa! That was a change. The first time we were there for communion was a disaster—for me. The communion service words were fine, the same ones I knew, but the actual serving was all wrong. Before the bread had been served to half the congregants, the cup was being started. You can't do that. Everyone gets served the bread before the cup is started. But wait, we're on a time schedule. We've got to be out of the sanctuary in an hour because the next service will be starting 30 minutes after. This wasn't working for either Jack or me. We moved to the Baptist church next door.

We were among friends. There were people from my home town and some from Jack's. It was warm and friendly. Women were participants in all facets of the church. Communion was traditional except now the glass cups were plastic and the metal trays were aluminum. We took youth trips again and had communion with goldfish and grapes. Life was good, and we were happy.

Eventually changes in church administration and leadership affected the feel of the church. We no longer found our spiritual needs being answered. Our next journey was a two-year long search for a new church home.

We found Wellspring. The people were friendly, the music was awesome, the location was perfect, the prayers were earnest, and communion was right. We were home.

I believe one of the greatest, but subtle jobs in this church is during communion. Communion servers know to look to the ushers to identify who needs to be served at their seat. No one is missed. Sunni, the pianist, gets served, and we get to sing acapella. We sound good. We are one. All who believe come to the table. No one who believes is excluded. It doesn't get any better than this. AMEN

But how is communion, the service, my story of HIStory? Well, my story is one of change and sharing, just as communion has changed and been shared.

Communion, by definition, is the sharing of thoughts or emotions, an intimate communication. It's talking with each other and sharing our celebrations and our devastations. It is sharing our beliefs, our doubts, and questions. It's helping a friend who is searching for answers and giving guidance through my faith and my story. My story is not yours, but maybe if you see what grounds me and makes me smile every day, it will give you pause to think of your journey and how you share it.

When I was working in healthcare, I found my faith to be the thing I could count on to get me through some wonderful and some horrible times. I marveled at the miracle of a perfect child being born—10 tiny fingers, lungs which functioned immediately, and tears of joy from happy parents. Oh, the happy prayers of thanksgiving and blessings received.

I would sing "Morning Has Broken" as I drove to work, and the sunrise greeted my day. I offered a prayer to guide my heart, my hands, and my mind as I gave each anesthetic. I asked prayers for those patients I hadn't met yet but would be a part of my day. May their surgeries and recoveries be uneventful. I was talking with God. We were singing. But there's another side.

I have spent a couple of nights in a lonely call room talking to God. There was a patient just down the hall from me. He had ALS, Lou Gehrig's disease. He had a young wife and no children. He couldn't hold his head up or feed himself. His brain functioned perfectly. He was dying, and he was only my age—36. I had to start his IV. How much time would it give him? Would he be comfortable?

God, you're not doing this to me. This is the conversation I had for hours—no sleep, no comfort, just talking and crying with God. I went home the next morning exhausted, because God and I had talked long into the night.

One night when I was on call, I was summoned to immediately report to the emergency room. A patient had suffered a catastrophic industrial burn to most of his body. It was a nightmare.

I had cared for two burn patients for a year during my time in anesthesia school as a Certified Registered Nurse Anesthetist. Their multiple anesthetics were difficult. I watched as their bodies contracted with scars, their family lives fell apart, and nothing was right for them again. Burns frighten my very core.

And now I had to confront this person who was dying. I had to be as professional as possible without giving an inkling of my terror. I had to ask this man, while he could still communicate, if there was anything he wanted me to share with family, friends, loved ones, and anyone who was not there. He would no longer be able to talk after I protected his airway. Could he, would he, share his last words with me? He did.

Again, I found the lonely, quiet, call room and talked with God—not to God, but *with* God. Actually, I think I did some yelling.

I had a conversation with God just as I would have talked with a friend. I actually spoke my words out loud and vented my fears, angst, fright, and sadness. I knew what the next few hours would mean as the toll of this accident took the life of this patient. I could envision the family as they got the news of a loved one so gravely hurt. Time was quickly passing for the chance to share a physical touch or words together.

I talked with God about the role I had played so briefly in this man's life, and yet he still stays in my mind's eye and in my heart. I cried and called out to God. He had put me in a position to share my skill and knowledge to care for others, but I hadn't agreed to this particular scenario. It was hard.

God knew this would test me, and I was angry with the test. I don't know if I passed it or just survived. Looking back, it was all in God's time and way. I am satisfied that I did my best.

My patient died the next day. Hopefully he was comfortable—physically and spiritually.

My faith and belief apparently were displayed at work other than in my talk sessions with God in the call room. I was asked to have prayers with patients who requested someone to pray with them. I didn't leave the patient, the family, or the church representative—minister, friend, deacon, Sunday school teacher, rabbi, Iman—when they requested time for prayer before going off to be the recipient of an anesthetic I was delivering. I asked to stay and be included, for them to offer a prayer for me, too. I loved it. It was so comforting. It was communing with God. My base of support, my foundation was there and being shared.

Now I believe my story of HIStory is to focus on our two grandchildren. They are not attending church as Jack and I did as children. Paige knows Baby Jesus lives in her heart and is love. We walk to find all the nativities we can at Christmas time. Logan learned the song "Jesus Loves Me." He was excited to be able to join the other children when they were asked to sing it at

Music Camp. He loved it. This is how I commune with God and grandchildren. This summer we'll read a Bible story everyday—not just 15 minutes of schoolwork or reading, but a Bible story too. I'm sharing the most important lesson they'll ever learn.

So, this is my part of HIStory. I hope my story is shared through my actions and my words. I don't think it is always. I strive to do better. It's like my journey through the service of communion: it has evolved, changed, but stayed the same. So has my communion with God and others. It's not so formal. The foundation is the same, but the road has changed, meandered, been paved, had potholes, and sometimes become a gravel path through the wood. But it's my story, and I've shared it with you.

Finding God in the Unexpected

by Mary Hatch

My journey in finding God and knowing He was guiding and watching over me, was comprised of people just showing up unexpectedly during a crisis time in my life.

It was 1998 at Swedish Hospital in Seattle, Washington. My husband, Alan, was admitted because his white cell count hit 100. Years earlier, Alan had been diagnosed with Non-Hodgkin's Lymphoma—he was only 48 years old. Alan had been treated in Mexico, where the doctors told us the cancer was gone.

Now we were put in a room in the emergency area and left to wait for quite a while. I got very cold and started to feel faint. A nurse checked my blood pressure; it had dropped to 75 over 50. The nurse brought in a cot for me to lie down on. She said she didn't know who to treat first. An hour later, my friend Terri, who happened to work in the emergency area, rushed into our room. She saw that Alan was critical, but she worried about me and told me I had to leave the room immediately. She wanted me to follow her for a cup of coffee and a cookie, but I didn't want to leave Alan. All she would say was that it was necessary for my health.

Terri guided me into the family waiting area, poured me a cup of coffee, and handed me a cookie. She would not leave until I ate something. When she saw I was doing as she said, she left the room and went back to check on Alan. After I finished, I hurried back to Al's room to be with him. Terri was in there. Because of Terri's urging, the nurse gave Alan a shot of Neupogen, which boosted the white cell count and revitalized his immune system. An hour later, he was coming around. A short time later, a nurse checked both our vitals and allowed me to take Alan home.

My friend Terri is a medical intuitive, and because of her gift, she has saved numerous lives over the years. As a medic in the Navy and then at Swedish Emergency, there were times when she just knew what was wrong and how to treat the patient. When Terri got off work later that night, she told me why she ushered me out of the room. She said when she entered Alan's room, she saw a white light like a shaft above his head. It appeared he was leaving this earth, and because I was so close to him, my body was failing. That's why she said I had to leave. She also told me that when I re-entered the room, the light above his head slowly closed.

Terri also relayed to me that it was probably no coincidence she was working that early. She said the regular person for that shift had called in sick, and the hospital had called her in as a replacement. I realized that it wasn't Al's time to be with God yet. God was giving me more precious time to be with Al and to have closure.

Months later, Alan was again admitted to the hospital because his white cell count was dangerously low. As Alan slept, the oncologist stopped in Alan's room. He told me that Alan was in the late stages of the lymphoma, and he wanted to give Alan more chemotherapy as part of their standard protocol. I told him that Alan wanted to die in peace and not go through more chemotherapy. The doctor was furious and marched out of the room.

I felt light-headed, and my knees were buckling. At that moment, my phone rang. It was my good friend Jackie calling to see if I was all right. She said she was worried about me. I knew in my heart God had prompted her at that exact moment to call me. I told her how grateful I was that she called and relayed my conversation with the doctor. She said she would pray for Alan and me and would be over to see me soon.

Alan passed away within the year, but there were many more small miracles that would lift our spirits above the despair and the sorrow.

God also sent His angels many times while I was caring for my elderly mother who had late stage dementia. One night, while living in North Carolina, I realized I was running low on groceries and drove to Food Lion with Mom. I realized I had forgotten her wheelchair and would have to leave her in the car while I went inside. I had done this before, so I knew I could leave her in the car for exactly 10 minutes. I raced around the store grabbing what I needed. While I was paying for the food, I saw my mother in the store. My heart started racing. There was a man kneeling down talking to her at her level, and a store manager was there with a phone in hand. I raced up to Mom. The lady store manager abruptly challenged me as to whether or not this elderly lady was my mom. I confirmed that she was. The manager seemed irritated as she told me she was just about to call 911 when this nice man stopped her and calmed Mom down.

The man introduced himself as a retired police officer. I could feel my heart pounding. I thought for sure I was going to jail for neglect. The man told me he understood that I was doing the best I could. My tears of relief started forming. He said when he was in law enforcement, he worked with caregivers and knew how hard it was. He assured me that I can't be everywhere all the time. He said Mom was just confused because it was night time. She had told him that she was looking for her mom. He said he knew that was me.

I explained to him that she would usually stay in the car for 10 minutes while I grabbed a few items. He said he understood. The store manager still seemed upset, but he calmed her down. He then turned to my mother and said, "Here's your daughter. She's going to take you home and make you a sandwich and some soup."

He followed us to the car and helped me buckle her in. I could barely hold back tears. I thanked him and told him he was a gift. He assured me things would be okay.

Over the six years that I cared for my mother, living angels were sent to me weekly. It was only through the grace of God I had the energy and stamina to care for my mother, whom I believe was also a living angel.

I found in my lifetime that God spoke to me: while walking in the forests (God's gardens); butterflies following my mother and me while strolling; friends calling when I was at my lowest; an in-home care giver I met in a laundry room at Mom's condo complex, whom I desperately needed and he turned out to be great; social workers entering my life at the right moment, changing my life for the better; and pastors that delivered that sermon I so desperately needed to give me hope and strengthen my faith. I found God everywhere, in everything, and in people. I just had to pay attention and to hear His still, small voice.

The Road to Methodism

By Elizabeth T. Jondahl

Whatever I have achieved in this life, I take little credit, for my star was hung not so much by my efforts but by the kind and generous spirit of people that gave me encouragement, an education, and a moral compass to follow. My success has been all the more remarkable as my ties to family were severed when I was a very young child, thus giving my rearing over to the "people of the village," at the Virginia Methodist Orphanage, my only home until I left after college.

Many years ago, on a warm day in June, I began a trek that has brought me to where I am today. I was the youngest of four children, three boys and myself, living in a remote rural section of Virginia where poverty was always sniffing at the door. With scant knowledge of the world around us, we knew very little of social status or who had what. Indeed, I had no recollection of ever being cold, hungry, or mistreated; I was part of a family, and I was loved.

Suddenly, everything familiar in our lives changed; our young father died, leaving Mama with four children, not a piece of property to her name, no skills beyond that of a homemaker, nor any insurance. Soon Mama became ill, and for a time, my siblings and I, like so many unwanted kittens, were sent to live with relatives and other near strangers. Somewhere along the way, my youngest brother contracted polio and help seemed in short supply. However, a kindly Methodist minister, whose church we sometimes attended, took our plight to heart and rescued us, in a manner of speaking. Soon the welfare department was notified, and the most important journey of my life was set in motion.

On the day of our departure, we were awakened very early, scrubbed from top to bottom, and with our meager belongings packed in two cardboard boxes, we stepped into a car which would take us away from all that was familiar. No relatives accompanied us, and I remember very little about the trip, except on that day my life was forever changed.

A year before Timmy and I arrived at the orphanage, my two older brothers were placed on a seven-hundred-acre farm in Quinton, Virginia, then owned by the Methodist Church. Along with fifty or so boys, they helped with farm chores that provided fresh produce and meat for the institution in Richmond where my youngest brother and I were taken that fateful day in June.

My first recollection of my new home, then called the Virginia Methodist Orphanage, was that of a large arched gate on two pillars and a tree-lined road. I didn't have a name for the seemingly long road then, but I later learned that it was simply called *The Lane*.

Left in Richmond, I quickly became part of new family, numbering nearly two hundred. The orphanage was a complex of large brick buildings and a few frame ones, separated by a main building. The facility was already quite old by the time I arrived, set just inside the city limits. In contrast to the city, fields anchored either side of the lane.

After completing my quarantine in the orphanage infirmary, I was placed in a cottage for younger girls.

Timmy, my brother, left shortly after our arrival to join our older brothers at the farm. His leaving came to symbolize the final dissolution of our family. My mother would visit us from time-to-time, though she never really got her life back together.

Each night, I sat with the other girls in the living room for devotions which included learning Bible verses and other religious instruction. Afterwards, without fail, we knelt by our beds and said our prayers silently, and like many children, I probably did more asking than seeking!

Singing was also a big part of our lives, and most of us were rather good at it. Later, when I was older, evening prayers often included singing songs from the *Cokesbury Hymnal*. I think many of us had it memorized by the time we were teenagers. At camp each summer, we often sang our blessings and ended the day with more singing.

In no time at all, I became immersed in my new life. While it was institutional living and training, it came to mean so much more. Slowly, changes came about that somewhat eroded the concept of the word *orphanage*. Most of these changes began when a new superintendent came on board. One day, as we walked up the lane from school, we noted that there was a new sign above the arches that read, "Virginia Methodist Children's Home." No longer did we feel stigmatized by the word *orphanage*, for there were very few children that were truly orphans.

Somewhere along the way, the old brick buildings began to disappear, replaced by modern housing. With all of these changes, we began to feel a sense of pride, much like children from intact families.

Over the years my gratitude to the Methodist church also grew for we saw and felt its goodness, not just from biblical teachings but in a myriad of tangible acts of kindness. The words *Methodist Church* seems to express some sort of giant corporation, but it is so much more. Good people saw a need to provide for children, surely the most vulnerable among its population. While The Methodist Conference in Virginia built the home, it was the effort of faceless lay people who breathed life into those brick buildings of long ago. Donations were given each December, known then as "Orphanage Month." We children sang in towns and villages across Virginia, our way of showing what the Methodist people of Virginia had accomplished.

Beginning with a Methodist minister and ending with the day I received my diploma from a Methodist college, I will always be grateful to the true spirit of Methodism. While I would never have picked an orphanage to replace the family I lost, it came to represent home to countless children over the years, the only home many of us would ever know.

The lane that led me to my new home so long ago would always be the road that began my early life. I walked many a mile up and down that lane, sometimes running and skipping, sometimes trudging, as all children do when the world appears to be upside-down. A child does not understand everything at once, and it would take countless years for me to realize that traveling up that lane on a warm day in June really was the best day of my life.

*Publisher's Note: Virginia's Methodist Children's Home has now become the United Methodist Family Services, caring for the needs of children, families, and communities. They are located in 10 cities throughout Virginia, providing residential treatment and specialized education, as well as foster care, adoption and community-based services. You can learn more at https://www.umfs.org/about/history/

One Thing Leads to Another

By Joyce Huffman

Stewardship and just saying yes, simply put, is what you do and why you do it. It's personal to each one of us and it's timeless. It is who we are and what we have become. Where do we go from here, and what are you willing to do?

Regarding that personal touch, many of you may know that I love reading stories, telling stories, and writing stories. Our Wellspring motto is WHAT IS YOUR STORY?

Over the last 60 years one of the most frequent requests from my grandchildren has been, "Grandma, tell us a story from the olden days when you were little." Keep in mind, we're talking the 1940s and World War II.

My mother, who suffered from poor health, often had to send me to church with a neighbor.

I didn't want to go without her. Along with assuring me I would be all right, she gave me a little responsibility of my own. Mom would wrap a dime in a handkerchief and put it in my pocket, so I wouldn't lose it. I was to place it in the offering basket. I loved putting my dime in the offering basket, and as I grew older I received my own offering envelopes. I was so proud; I felt it was an honor. By that time the going minimum wage was 50 cents per hour, and I was earning some money in various chores. Up to a dollar a week!

Remember, back then the bulletins were typed on a full-size piece of paper, and the back of the bulletin listed givers in denomination categories: $10, $20, $30, etc. I leave it to your imagination as to which part of the bulletin was widely read—even by children. "Wow, did you see what Dr. Downey gave? Twenty dollars!" My name never made it to the back of the bulletin, but I always *wanted* to. In retrospect, when I consider what I earned and what I gave, I was tithing. I just didn't know it.

Now let's forward to the 1960s. My husband, Bob, was Lay Leader at our church in Pennsylvania, and he had asked his college professor, Dr. Bowlen, to speak on tithing. I remember his message but most clearly this line, "It will not make you rich, but you will always have enough."

That day Bob and I went home, talked, and decided to commit to a lifetime of tithing. And it's true, we're not rich, but we have enough.

This story has such a rewarding ending as my time line moves forward to the 1990s in Williamsburg. One early morning I started thinking, and it occurred to me that I had never told that story to Dr. Bowlen. So, I took a chance that he might still be alive, and I wrote him an overdue thank you letter—30 years overdue!

Dr. Bowlen wrote back and thanked *me*. He never knew how or if anyone ever responded to his message, so he loved getting that letter. I had made his day, and he had made my day by his response. That was the best letter I ever wrote and best reply I ever received.

I wrote this testimony when I had written 40 letters in 40 days as my Lenten challenge. It was a stewardship gift of my time and what I was willing to do. I planned to stop here, but then I received a letter from an older parishioner staying in assisted living who had responded to a letter I had written. This one sentence now takes second place only to Dr. Bowlen's letter. "Joyce, it's so nice to receive an envelope that does not have a window."

Dimes in a basket. A long overdue thank you. Envelopes without windows. ONE THING LEADS TO ANOTHER WHEN YOU SAY YES.

Saved by Angels

by Bob Corson

I am a child of God and a loyal and devoted follower of my Lord and Savior Jesus Christ. I am recovering from the effects of being an Adult Child of an Alcoholic resulting in alcohol abuse, food abuse, and sexual addiction.

I was born in Brooklyn, New York, the City of Churches and the home of the Brooklyn Dodgers baseball team. Yes, for those people born after 1945, there was an awesome major league baseball team in Brooklyn until 1957 with an amazing second baseman by the name of Jackie Robinson, and I was their biggest fan.

I was part of a highly dysfunctional family. My father was an abusive, chronic alcoholic, and my mother was his enabler. Growing up, I was in constant fear for myself, my sister, and my mother. Due to my father's drinking, we moved regularly. I attended three grammar schools, two junior high schools, and two high schools.

The constant moving and having to make new friends every-other-year did little for my emotional and psychological development. I joined a street gang and had several encounters with the police, along with several overnights in the local jail.

When I was 12, my mother told me I had been adopted. I was told nothing was known about my biological parents as I was left abandoned on the hospital steps. This also didn't help my development. I started drinking at 15 and was an alcoholic by 17.

I fell in love with a beautiful Italian girl named Grace who lived next door to us. Her parents were old-school and dating anyone who wasn't Italian was not an option. I was of Irish decent, the worst possible nationality to Italians. They believed all "Irishers" were a bunch of drunks.

Grace and I managed to sneak away on several occasions. One night we were necking on lover's lane in my car. I looked in the rearview mirror and there was her father in his car behind us. I hit the gas pedal and took off to parts unknown. We discussed going to Maryland to get married, but we came to our senses and went home.

From my bedroom, I heard the yelling and screaming coming from her house. The following day I was called to her cousin's house who lived down the street. Her cousin told me I could never see her again. I was destroyed. Several months later, I joined the Army to get away.

I had problems in the service due to my upbringing. I was court-martialed twice but, thanks to God and an awesome Army Chaplain who He called on to defend me, I was not imprisoned and even received an Honorable Discharge after fulfilling my two-year obligation.

At age 25, my drinking problem came to a head during my bachelor party. I got so drunk, I was hospitalized with alcohol poisoning. From then on, just the smell of alcohol would get me sick. God works in strange ways.

The lovely young girl was still willing to marry me, and we had two great children.

However, my experience as an Adult Child of an Alcoholic created problem in the marriage. One of the classic behaviors of an ACOA is not telling the truth. As a child, telling the truth resulted in severe consequences and pain inflicted on me by my father, so I had a hard time being truthful when I did something wrong.

Because of my mother and father's constant fighting, as a child, I spent many nights hiding in a closet. That translated to being unable to deal with conflict as an adult. I was unable to cope with any arguing in my marriage.

Due to the stress following arguments with my wife, I developed cardiac arrhythmia and spent many nights in the emergency room. As you can imagine, arguing is the national pastime of Italians. The marriage suffered as a result.

My mother had chronic emphysema. When she was near death, she told me that my biological mother was her sister, my Aunt Georgia. While I was shocked, I was not surprised. Georgia was my favorite relative, and I was closer to her than my adopted parents, although she was not in my life often because she, like her Irish brothers and sisters, was a chronic alcoholic.

I was 54 when Aunt Georgia and I met for the first time as mother and son at my adopted mother's funeral. There were both tears of joy at the reconciliation and tears of sadness due to my adopted mother's death.

I learned a lot more about Aunt Georgia after that. My maternal grandmother had seven children. Her first husband abandoned the family early. When she remarried, her new husband demanded the children go to orphanages. Orphanages in the 1920s were not the best place to be. Georgia and her younger sister went hungry many nights. One night, Georgia's younger sister ate rat poison, thinking it was food. She died in Georgia's arms. Imagine the impact this had on the young Georgia.

When Georgia left the orphanage at 16, she turned to alcohol to ease her pain. One evening she was gang raped, resulting in my eventual birth. Unable to care for a child, she gave me to her older sister Florence, my adoptive mother, who could not bear children. The sisters agreed that I would not be told about my birth until one of them was near death. Georgia was always there for my birthdays and Christmas. How painful it must have been for her.

She worked as a maid at the Yale Club in New York City. After several years, she was promoted to supervisor because of her caring behavior towards residents and staff. She worked part-time as a school cafeteria worker, frequently using her own money to supplement the food allowance to provide a healthier appetizing meal for her "children."

Eventually Georgia retired with a small pension. She lived in a supported housing development in New Jersey and was always helping older residents needing extra care. They called her the Angel of Bergen County. She became president of the tenants' association and lobbied fearlessly to improve the residents' quality of life.

Georgia remained a chronic alcoholic until her 60th birthday when she was born again in the Christian faith and began her recovery with Alcoholics Anonymous. She was a sponsor for many women.

One evening at an AA function, she fell to the floor with a massive stroke. Her hospital room was filled with cards and flowers from AA members, neighbors, and school children who wanted to know when Miss Georgia would return. She never did.

My mother died two years after the stroke. Her ashes sit on the mantel in our living room. I share her story because I am a product of her Christianity and her recovery. I hope that her story will inspire others as it continually does me. I pray I will impact as many people's lives as she did.

Getting back to my story, after my children left home, my marriage deteriorated. I fought with everyone, including my sister and my children. I was unemployed, depressed, abusing depression medication, addicted to sex and pornography, and cheating on my wife. I began drinking again.

One night I decided to end it all. I bought some weights, consumed a bottle of gin, and headed to the fishing pier at Rehoboth Beach in Delaware to drown myself. As I walked to the end of the pier, there in front of me was an angelic vision of Georgia shaking her head no. I fell to my knees and began weeping.

Suddenly a man came behind me and helped me up. It was a Delaware State Trooper who saw my car weaving down route 13 and watched me pull into the parking lot at a strange hour, so he followed me. His name was Jim Clark. We talked, and he told me he understood. We went to McDonalds for coffee. He followed me all the way to a psychiatric hospital where I was admitted.

I tried to call him after I was released but was told there was no trooper there by that name nor anyone that fit the description. I called the county police and the local sheriff's office looking for him but to no avail. Today I still wonder who or what came to my rescue. Was it an angel or Jesus Christ? The trooper's initials were JC.

"For he will command his angels concerning you to guard you in all your ways." (Psalm 91:11)

Following the hospitalization, I asked my wife for a divorce, and she agreed to it. In 2008, I remarried, was born again, and my life changed. My beautiful wife Pat, her children, and her grandchildren are devout Christians who love me as one of their own.

I was baptized in the river, and the feeling I had during the process cannot be explained other than to say it was other-worldly. I have become a disciple and an active member of our church. I sing in the choir, serve as a liturgist, and perform Christian magic for the children. I participate in mission trips when I can, and I will become a member of the Stephen's Ministry in January. They, along with Jesus and my biological daughter, have saved me, and I am deeply indebted.

I have taken a 12-step program as an ACOA and was on the leadership team of Celebrate Recovery at our church in Florida and a church in Williamsburg, Virginia. I practice the twelfth step with this statement: *"Having had a spiritual awakening as a result of these steps, I try to carry this message of recovery to others and practice these principals in all my affairs."*

I want to share with you one of Georgia's favorite motivational poems. Note that where the original poem refers to the *SUN*, I have changed it to the *SON*, Jesus Christ. If you ever reach the point where you are "at the end of the pier" as I was, I hope you will recall this story and this simple little poem and ask Georgia for help. I assure you she will listen.

The teensy-weensy spider climbed up the water spout.
Down came the rain and washed the spider out.
Then came the Son who dried up all the rain,
And the teensy-weensy spider climbed up the spout again.
I know nothing stays the same, but if you put Jesus Christ in the game,
Things will turn around again

"For You, O Lord, are my hope, my trust, O LORD, from my youth." (Psalm 71:5)

What Does Jesus Look Like?

By Beth Burroughs

When Edward first proposed that we tell our stories, I, too, waited for everyone else to queue up with their wonderful sagas. I thought mine is quite ordinary, and, in places, private—known only to God and me. So, I decided to just listen to everyone else bare his or her soul from the lectern. Then Ronda Williams offered her story, and I immediately dismissed any thoughts of sharing, as hers was the best there could be.

Then a couple of other folks came along and told just a part of their journey. I decided that I could do a <u>part</u> of my journey. And that wouldn't be so bad. So, I'd like to tell you of a part of my spiritual journey of the past 10 years: my 'going to prison' experience.

Several times in the past seven years I've announced to our Sunday School class, "Well, I'm going to prison next Saturday." To which someone will mutter, "So! They finally caught up with you, eh?" And we all get a good laugh.

A little more than 10 years ago a good friend from our previous church in Hampton sadly revealed to us that his son had been arrested, was awaiting trial, and it "looked bad." Later he said that the son had been sentenced to prison for a "looooonnnnnng time." I don't remember if he asked or I volunteered, but we determined that I would write to the young man. I had met the son but didn't really know him. All I know is his dad asked a favor. I was glad to oblige.

His name is Joe.

First, Joe was sent to Green Rock Correctional Center, in Chatham, Virginia, north of Danville. About a year after he got to Green Rock, he and his girlfriend got married in the prison. She had been with him for at least a couple of years, and she is still truly dedicated to him. He and I wrote once or twice monthly. After a while, his dad told me Joe couldn't read my handwriting, so I started typing my letters. I used decorated stationery to try to bring in a little difference and maybe joy.

A few years later he was transferred to Greensville Correctional Center, in Jarratt, Virginia, north of Emporia. Closer than Green Rock. Both Green Rock and Greensville are level 2 - 3 security prisons. Lifers are there. They have nothing to lose. Greensville is where the executions are held in Virginia. At both of those facilities, life is an exercise in self-preservation. Every day. We just cannot imagine.

The last year Joe was at Greensville, they were allowed to start receiving email, and the prisoners could buy devices to receive email. We now email two or three times a month, and I send e-cards. I still do mail by post occasionally, if I want to send pictures.

When he was at Greensville, I began going with Joe's wife, Davida, to see him. I drive to Hampton to pick her up at her home, three or four times a year, on a Saturday.

Now I just want to tell a little about my prison experience.

We must be approved to visit, which involved an application and background check. In Greensville, we could not wear any jewelry except wedding rings, no watches, no earrings, no precious metals or stones. We had two or three pat downs, shoes off, went through a metal detector, nothing in pockets, nothing in mouth, no gum, no tissues (hard for me), could not carry anything in or out. If you needed a sweater in the visitation room, you wore it in and wore it out. I had to surrender my ID card and my car keys, and then retrieve them on the way out.

Once in the visitation room, the prisoners sat facing a raised dais/desk, behind which sit two or three correctional officers. Prisoners are strip-searched both before and after visits. Still, despite many precautions, lots of drug smuggling passes through the visitation room. It was a big room with high ceilings and nothing to absorb sound. The noise was terrible.

I've been there at Count Time. That's when the whistle blows, prisoners stand, wait until CO comes around with clip board, state their name and ID number, then sit. Visitors don't talk or move during count.

When sending mail, it was restricted to letters and cards only. His name and ID number had to be on every page. Envelopes are opened, examined, and separated from mail. I've never had anything censored that I know of, but we are always warned that it can happen. I have had cards returned because they were multiple layered. With emails, we are warned that the submissions are read, and objectionable material deleted. No packages, gifts, or money can be sent directly. I can order books sent to him through Amazon. Snack foods may be ordered and delivered only through an approved company. Money is sent to a company that puts it in his account. I also send Joe magazines through Prison Fellowship—Upper Room, Reader's Digest, couple of sporting magazines, and Popular Mechanics.

Joe has been in a gang while in prison and also in solitary confinement, *the hole*. If I didn't hear from him for a while, finally he would write that he was in *the hole*—sometimes it was days, sometimes maybe three to four weeks. He said his longest stay was two months for something his cellmate had in the cell that could have been used as a weapon. Joe was put in *the hole* for various offenses, some of which he says he did, some he claims he did not. I don't know. I don't ask. I don't want to know.

He has tattoos all over his body from the neck down. I only see his arms and neck. He tells me the rest is covered. He promised his dad he wouldn't have any ink from the neck up, and he has honored that promise. The ink is not ink, but actually ashes from burned objects. I don't ask. I don't want to know how or what they burn to make that. I don't want to know what they use as needles. Some gang tats are inked over or changed away from offensive signs or words. There is no way for them to be removed while in prison. I'm told me that prison tats will fade in time, as the soot will eventually be absorbed into his body. But some of the plastics burned to make the ash solidifies and stays under the skin.

About two and a half years ago, Joe was transferred to St. Bride's Correctional Center in Chesapeake, Virginia. That is a level 1-2 center. Men there tend to be less violent, usually have five-year sentences, or five or less years yet to serve. They have a few more freedoms, and there is a slightly different attitude among the correctional officers.

When Joe transferred to St. Bride's, he brought with him a book (I'm guessing gang related) that was allowed at Greensville but is not allowed at St. Bride's. Because he had that book among his possessions, he lost six months of good behavior time that he will never recover.

Because it is minimum security, there is only one pat down. I have to take my shoes off, but I can keep the car keys. There are fewer metal gates clanging shut before the next one mysteriously chugs open. We are still always being watched.

Joe joined the Catholic Church after he got to St. Bride's. He turned his life around and proved himself to be trustworthy. He is allowed to work outside, but only on the compound. He's now in classes to learn life skills and a trade to prepare him for life outside. Joe has just about always had a job of some kind—cleaning toilets, scrubbing walls or floors, sweeping, or most anything. Prisoners earn 25-30 cents an hour. Because he has proven himself, he is now in a job that earns what he says is the top wage in prison—40 cents an hour. He works in the prison commissary inventorying food, stocking, unloading trucks, and preparing trays. He likes this and would like to do it after he is released.

Not all of that 40 cents an hour goes to him. A percentage goes to his personal savings account which will be given to him when he is released. Some goes to back child support for his son. Some goes toward back court costs. Prisoners must buy some personal hygiene items and any extra clothing they want. So being in prison does cost them money; everything is not paid for. He has a phone and calls Davida every night. She pays for the minutes on his phone.

In St. Bride's, Joe finally found God's dwelling place, and to him, God's dwelling place is lovely. At last, he is in the Courts of the Lord. When I read Psalm 84, I knew it applies to Joe now, and I pray that it continues to do so. He is so much more assured of his salvation, confident in God's love, and confident that his sins are forgiven. He is much less rebellious and defensive. Joe knows he's a child of God and is ever so grateful for God's love for him.

Joe is now looking to the future. He still has no idea of what life on the outside will look like. His original sentence was 28 years. He will serve 13, with another 15 on probation. His crime was armed robbery and car-jacking, in a single incident. He can never own a gun. He will be able to fish, maybe bow hunt, but no gun hunting. Joe and Davida will be in counseling for a long time for him to adjust to life on the outside.

Joe expects, looks forward to, and counts the days until February 2019 and his release from prison.

This story is not about explaining prison life. It's about glorifying God and Jesus Christ His Son, who came to earth so that we could learn more about God the Father.

So where is Jesus in this? To me, Jesus is a 31-year-old, tattooed prisoner. Joe has taught me so much. Humility, gratitude, perseverance, and strength, among other things.

Let's look at Romans 6:5-6 for a minute. *For if we have been united with him in a death like his, we will certainly be united with him in a resurrection like his. We know that our old self was crucified with him so that the body of sin might be destroyed, and we might no longer be enslaved to sin.*

Can you imagine life in prison for more than a third of your life so far? And your very life reminding you—every minute, every breath—of your sin against society? And then to imagine the leap Joe had to take to accept Christ into his life, die to sin, leave the gangs and swastikas behind, and accept Christ's love for him. That would be sort of like jumping the Grand Canyon in your puddle boots. Though he will pay the consequences for the rest of his life, his guilt has been forgiven by God. Gone. He died to sin and is alive in Christ.

To Joe, Jesus on earth is his priest and a 77-year-old grandmother. My continued, God-like love has brought him to Jesus. He knows I love him no matter what. He knows I don't like everything he does and says, and I know he lies to me. But I always told him that God loves him, and I love him. Now he believes it. His family has been sporadic in their visits and contacts. They have their own problems, and it's difficult for them to affirm him.

I would never have thought this experience would be a part of my life. When I offered a casual "sure," to a broken-hearted plea from a dad those years ago, I had no idea where it would take me and how it would grow me. I certainly would not have chosen this experience, but I'm ever so grateful to have had it. I have no idea how it will impact the rest of my life, but God knows.

I know Joe wants to go to schools, churches, clubs, and anywhere there is someone to listen to impress upon them to never repeat the experience he has had these last 10-13 years. And if I can prevent one person from ever having to live this life, I will be glad to do that.

Now that I have gone through this experience, I can help some folks live with a loved one's prison time and know what to expect on their visits. I'll be glad to talk with anyone about anything I have experienced and learned over the past 10 years.

Now Joe is *under a year*. After 12 years in prison, Joe couldn't imagine that this day would really come. He is busy taking classes and training to help him live on the outside. He is extra careful not to do or say anything that would get him in trouble and extend his time. His family and I are so excited at the anticipation of his release. I'm making him a special quilt to mark the occasion.

God is good!
All the time!
And all the time!
God is good!
Amen

God's Will

By Gail Scullion

My story began as a child. I was blessed to be born into a Christian family where I was taught as a little girl the love of God and how He gave His only son to die for us so that we could be saved. Our whole life was centered around church—our own and the ones where my Pap would preach. At the young age of three, I went with my grandfather on Sunday afternoons to sing with him at his three charges. The congregations were teeming with such a wonderful, kind, Spirit-filled people. There were no choirs—often no accompanying music at all; we would just sing. Some of them only had 20 people or so.

At the age of 13, I accepted Christ as my Savior at a Billy Graham crusade at the Civic

Arena in Pittsburgh. My grandfather was one of the volunteer ministers at the alter call. Pap came up to me and I will never forget what he said. "Honey, I am so proud of you for your decision, but I want you to know this doesn't mean you are on easy street. The devil will be on you hot and heavy to sway you and try to take you away from God."

Through the years, I continued to sing, first with the junior choir, then the senior choir. In the 1960s, we did the unthinkable and sang with a 12-string guitar. My brother, a very good friend named Cathy, and I started the group "We Three." We sang all over the tri-state area for three years with Bishop Roy C. Nichols. What an awesome privilege and experience for us.

In 1973, my world came crashing down when my daddy died during open heart surgery at the young age of 56. He was our rock, a lieutenant colonel in the Army Reserve, a school teacher, a lay minister, and a soft-spoken but hugely respected mentor to many young people. Growing up, our house was where all the kids would hang out. Mom and dad had an open-door policy; come on in and stay for supper. All of our friends loved them. We were blessed.

I was always told if you prayed and you believed, God would answer your prayers, but one important fact I didn't get was it had to be God's will. Daddy's death rocked my faith walk. I almost lost my way, but God got me to understand. Once again, we walked together. At a point when I was so angry and felt betrayed, I remember saying to Nanny, "I'm so mad at God." She cautioned me not to say that. I told her that He always knows what's in my heart, so He already knows I'm angry anyway.

I have always been able to just talk to God. He's my best friend, but that was a rough time for me. Through the years, my faith matured, and my life went on.

I met and married a wonderful man who I have been with for 40 years. He is a born-again Christian and has been a wonderful father to our girls and an awesome Pap and Papa to our grandchildren and great-grandchildren.

I have had other heartaches and losses. I lost both my parents at a young age and my 15-month-old granddaughter Meagan in 1987. That, without a doubt, was the hardest thing we ever had to go through—the death of a child. But God helped us through it all.

God has blessed me in so many ways with family and love. I owe everything I am and have to Him. I thank my family for giving me the strong foundation of my Christian faith. I wouldn't want to live a day without my loving Lord. I truly don't know how individuals make it without Him. I praise Him for the gift of music He has given me to help share my love and praise for Him throughout my life with others. Thank you, Lord.

When the Moon Blocked out the Son

By Debbie Noonan

During my high school years in Methodist Youth Fellowship, I met many wonderful people with whom I spent many amazing spiritual hours. We studied the Bible together and came to understand our Methodist religion to the best of each of our individual abilities. We were all walking the same or similar paths. Or so I thought.

During my senior year of college, I ran into one of my Methodist Youth Fellowship friends on campus passing out materials and talking up a new spiritual experience that he'd had and wanted everyone to have. All you had to do was come to a weekend retreat and learn about this new, exciting religion. Supposedly, one would not have to give up one's old beliefs by going on this retreat. This new religion would be an extension, a renewal, a way to grow in one's own belief system.

I was in a period of my life where I was questioning where I was going, what was next, and where exactly religion fit into my life. I thought this would be an interesting weekend getaway, a chance to meet some new people, and yes, find out something new. So, I went.

In the beginning it was all very exciting. Everyone was very kind. They spoke endlessly about how the Bible spoke of a second coming and how this was the time. They read Scripture that pointed this out and supported their words. It all seemed so clear and so true. It all made so much sense. It wasn't until the end of the weekend that they told us they were followers of the Reverend Sun Myung Moon and the Unification Church, better known as Moonies.

We left about noon on Sunday, and I went home and told my mother all about it. I was so excited. It made so much sense, how could it not be true? I was ready to jump into this new religion feet first. This scared my mother to death. She immediately called another of my Methodist Youth Fellowship friends from high school who was currently attending Methodist seminary, and she told him to come pick me up, which he did.

I spent the rest of the afternoon with him during which time I explained what I had been taught, and he attempted to debunk it all. We talked and cried and laughed and cried and talked continually. I showed him the Scriptures that they quoted me and how this pointed to Moon being the second coming of Christ. He would then show me another Scripture that showed an opposing view. After about five hours, he was able to convince me that all their teachings were truly bogus, that it was a cult, and that I was lucky to have gotten out of there, but it did take all or more of the five hours to do so.

I was very lucky to have met both of these friends during high school Methodist Youth Fellowship. It was very strange how different their spiritual paths diverged and how they both affected me so deeply when I was in a questioning time in my life. I'm thankful things worked out as they did. I don't know what happened to my friend who joined the Unification Church. I hope he found fulfillment in his beliefs. But his beliefs were not for me. I'm still in contact with my other friend some 45 years later.

My journey with God has always been a difficult and wavering one. I always know He's there when I need Him, watching over me, guiding me, and when I have questions I know I can turn to Him for answers. In this instance, He was there again, watching me, guiding me (and my mother), making sure we followed the correct path. It was important that I met both of these individuals because they showed me how important God is in my life; the Moonie showed me that I was searching for something—anything—and of course, the seminarian showed me that the Moonies were not the right answer.

The Bible is full of different and often contradictory passages. Different religions pick and choose the ones that fit their beliefs or twist certain passages to make them fit their beliefs. For me, Christianity is about love and "doing unto others as you would have them do unto you."

No Ah-ha Moment

By Dawn Brotherton

I always felt cheated that I never had an "ah-ha" moment.

I've heard people tell their stories of how they found Christ and experienced their ah-ha moment, when their eyes were opened to Christ for the first time.

I have never *not* known Christ. Even though my family didn't go to church growing up, both my parents believed in God and talked about him in a matter-of-fact way. The idea that He may not exist was never a consideration.

When I was in grade school, I went to Bible study after school with my two older sisters. It was actually held in one of the classrooms of the public school building. I don't know which church ran the program, but I looked forward to it. I remember doing Bible drills. We would all hold our Bibles in the air. The leader would call out a Bible verse. The person that found the right page and started reading the verse aloud first won. I'm not even sure what we won, but it was a fun way to get to know how to find things in the Bible.

Eventually I started going to church with my neighbors. It was a small Lutheran church in Champion, Ohio. In fifth grade I was baptized. In eighth grade I went through confirmation. By high school I was on the church council as the youth representative. I was very active in choir and youth group.

It wasn't all roses. There was one parent that always looked down on my younger sister and I because we didn't wear dresses to church. I was all tomboy, and dresses weren't part of my wardrobe. She didn't like her boys associating with us and wouldn't let us sit together. It wasn't that she was mean. She just had a different idea of what was proper for church.

The neighbors that took us to church with them loved us unconditionally and always thanked us for going with them to church—no matter what we were wearing.

In college, I didn't go looking for a church to attend. I would go when I was home, but not at school. My junior year, I received a "D" in Calculus IV and was on the verge of losing my ROTC math scholarship. I needed someone to talk to.

I searched the phone book to find a Lutheran church. The pastor was wonderful. He took the time to talk me through the options and helped me get my life in order. I switched majors, accepted a missile-launch officer scholarship, and was back on track to graduate with only one extra semester. I got very involved with the church again and even became the sexton to earn some extra money. I enjoyed having the church to myself at times.

Through my many duty stations in my 28-year Air Force career, I moved and found different churches. I was never stuck on any denomination. I selected a Christian church that felt right.

I met my husband when I was stationed in Korea in 1993. He was an Air Force fighter pilot in the squadron I worked for. Within two weeks we were dating exclusively, and within four months we were talking about marriage. During one of those talks, it came out that the love of my life didn't believe in God. I was crushed. It seemed unbelievable that we could have so much in common, believe in so many of the same things, want to raise our children the same way, but he didn't care about the most important thing in my life. I immediately started back pedaling and decided there was no way we could be married. He claimed to be agnostic, not atheist, so everything would be fine. He was also baptized in a Lutheran church, and his mother took him until they moved when he was about eight (his dad was an atheist). I asked what he would do when our children asked him about God. He said he would tell them to ask their mother.

In the end, he convinced me. And I clung to the Bible verse that says a husband would be sanctified through his wife's belief. I thought I could believe enough for both of us.

In Las Vegas, I was the youth director for the church. My husband would help me with field trips or anything I asked him to do. In Germany, I established a lending library for the church. It was many hours painting, building shelves, moving boxes or books, and manning the desk. My husband helped through it all. He would even meet me for lunch after church and ask me about the sermon. Our base chaplain was great and told wonderful stories. The chaplain and his wife came to our house regularly for dinners or parties, and my husband really enjoyed talking to him. But he wouldn't go to church.

We have two beautiful daughters who attend church with me regularly. It was never an option for them growing up, even though Daddy "got to" stay home. My oldest daughter was baptized in Cibolo, Texas in a Lutheran church. My husband had to attend classes with me leading up to the baptism. He had to stand in front of the church and promise to raise our daughter in the Christian faith. I thought for sure this was the turning point: when my prayers would be answered, and my husband would accept God. Not so much. Nothing changed.

Our second daughter was baptized in the same Lutheran church in Ohio that was I was baptized in. Again, my husband stood at the front of the church and made a promise before God to raise her Christian.

In Newport News, Virginia, the girls and I attended a non-denominational church. I set up a thrift store and my husband designed and built the racks to hang the clothes. We made many good friends in the congregation and would get together socially often. Again, I thought—this is it. He's going to see how important God is.

As the girls grew and became stronger in their faith, my husband became more argumentative. He would make negative comments about church, religion, and any one that believed in Christ. We had full-blown arguments when I reminded him that he promised to keep his mouth shut about anything religious. Instead of getting closer to God, he was fighting it harder. I just knew it was the devil at work, warring to keep my husband on his side and away from God. I continued to pray and be faithful that he would choose wisely. He is a loyal husband and good father in all things but this one.

The girls continued to flourish. They became active in the church and both received confirmation at Wellspring Methodist Church in Williamsburg, Virginia. My husband and I have been married 24 years. It's hard to understand why God won't grant my prayer and open my husband's heart. Throughout the Bible there are times when God "hardens the heart" of certain people in order to display God's power or make a point. I feel like that is what He has done in this situation. I know belief in Him is free-will, but it is so tiring at times to constantly battle against my husband for God. I dream of the day he will enjoy going to church with me, and we can share thoughts about the sermon afterwards. I want to be able to openly praise God without a negative comment. I want my girls to feel comfortable and secure in their beliefs, without their father continually trying to tear down their walls.

I pray for my husband's ah-ha moment.

Share Your Story

God wants us to proclaim the good news of His love. Openly tell others what you have learned along your faith walk.

It isn't all going to be rainbows and sunshine. God didn't promise that our lives would be easy, but He did promise that we would never be alone.

He will be with us in tough times, arms outstretched for a loving embrace. No matter what we face, He will be our Father.

Go forth with your arms outstretched, giving the loving embrace to those who need it. Share your story and your Christian love.

www.ingramcontent.com/pod-product-compliance
Lightning Source LLC
Chambersburg PA
CBHW021443080526
44588CB00009B/670